Contents

British Library Cataloguing in Publication Data
First songs
   1. Children's songs in English — Collections
  I. Finnigan, Helen   II. Langton, Roger   III. Series
784.6'2406
  ISBN 0-7214-1122-3

First edition

Published by Ladybird Books Ltd Loughborough Leicestershire UK
Ladybird Books Inc Auburn Maine 04210 USA

Printed in England

Ladybird Action Rhymes

First songs

compiled by Helen Finnigan
illustrated by Roger Langton

Ladybird Books

Clap-a, clap-a, handies,
Mummy's at the well.
Daddy's gone to London,
To buy Baby a bell.

Ride a cock horse
To Banbury Cross,
To see a fine lady
Upon a white horse.
With rings on her fingers
And bells on her toes,
She shall have music
Wherever she goes.

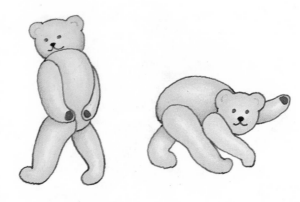

Teddy bear, teddy bear, turn around,
Teddy bear, teddy bear, touch the ground.
Teddy bear, teddy bear, show your dirty shoe,
Teddy bear, teddy bear, that will do.

Teddy bear, teddy bear, climb upstairs,
Teddy bear, teddy bear, say your prayers.
Teddy bear, teddy bear, turn off the light,
Teddy bear, teddy bear, say goodnight.

Pat-a-cake, pat-a-cake,
Baker's man,
Bake me a cake
As fast as you can.
Pat it and prick it
And mark it with 'B',
And put it in the oven
For Baby and me.

Bye, Baby Bunting,
Daddy's gone a-hunting.
Gone to get a rabbit skin,
To wrap Baby Bunting in.

Rock-a-bye baby, on the tree top,
When the wind blows the cradle will rock.
When the bough breaks, the cradle will fall.
Down will come baby, cradle and all.

See-saw, Margery Daw,
Jenny shall have a new master.
She shall have but a penny a day,
Because she can't work any faster.

Trot, trot, trot,
Go and never stop.
Trudge along, my little pony,
Where 'tis rough and where 'tis stony.
Go and never stop,
Trot, trot, trot, trot, trot.

Dance to your daddy,
My bonnie laddie,
Dance to your daddy,
My bonnie lamb.

You shall get a fishy,
In a little dishy,
You shall get a fishy,
When the boat comes in.

You shall get a coatie,
And a pair of breekies,
And you'll get an eggy,
And a bit of ham.

You shall get a pony,
Fit to ride for ony,
And you'll get a whippy,
For to make him gang.

Dance to your daddy,
My bonnie laddie,
Dance to your daddy,
My bonnie lamb.

Peek-a-boo, peek-a-boo,
Who's that hiding there?
Peek-a-boo, peek-a-boo,
Peter's behind the chair.

(Change name as required.)

This little pig went to market,
This little pig stayed at home.
This little pig had roast beef,
This little pig had none.
And this little pig said, "Wee, wee, wee, wee,"
All the way home.

Jack in the box
Quiet as a mouse
Curled up asleep
In his own little house.

Knock on the lid
Give it a bump
Waken him up
And out he'll jump.

"Pussy cat, Pussy cat,
  where have you been?"
"I've been up to London
  to look at the Queen."
"Pussy cat, Pussy cat,
  what did you there?"
"I frightened a little mouse
  under her chair."

Pease porridge hot,
Pease porridge cold,
Pease porridge in the pot,
Nine days old.
Some like it hot,
Some like it cold,
Some like it in the pot,
Nine days old.

house

windows

This is my little house,
This is the door.
The windows are shining,
And so is the floor.

door

floor

chimney

Outside there's a chimney,
As tall as can be,
With smoke that goes curling up.
Come and see!

smoke

Miss Polly had a dolly
Who was sick, sick, sick.
So she phoned for the doctor
To be quick, quick, quick.

The doctor came
With his bag and his hat,
And he rapped at the door
With a rat-tat-tat.

He looked at the dolly
And he shook his head.
Then he said, "Miss Polly,
Put her straight to bed."

He wrote on a paper
For a pill, pill, pill.
"I'll be back in the morning
With my bill, bill, bill."

Wee Willie Winkie
Runs through the town,
Upstairs and downstairs,
In his nightgown,
Rapping at the windows,
Crying through the locks,
"Are all the children in their beds?
It's past 8 o'clock!"

The wheels on the bus go round and round,
Round and round, round and round.
The wheels on the bus go round and round,
All day long.

The horn on the bus goes peep, peep, peep,
Peep peep peep, peep peep peep.
The horn on the bus goes peep peep peep,
All day long.

The windscreen wiper on the bus goes
    swish, swish, swish,
Swish swish swish, swish swish swish.
The windscreen wiper on the bus goes
    swish swish swish,
All day long.

The people on the bus bounce up and down,
   up and down, up and down.
The people on the bus
   bounce up and down,
All day long.

The lights on the bus go
   twinkle, twinkle, twinkle,
Twinkle twinkle twinkle, twinkle twinkle twinkle.
The lights on the bus go
   twinkle twinkle twinkle,
All day long.

Hush, little baby, don't say a word!
Mummy's going to buy you
   a mocking bird.
And if that mocking bird don't sing,
Mummy's going to buy you
   a diamond ring.
And if that diamond ring turns to brass,
Mummy's going to buy you
   a looking glass.
And if that looking glass gets broke,
Mummy's going to buy you
   a billy goat.
And if that billy goat won't pull,
Mummy's going to buy you
   a cart and bull.
And if that cart and bull turn over,
Mummy's going to buy you
   a dog called Rover.
And if that dog called Rover won't bark,
Mummy's going to buy you
   a horse and cart.
And if that horse and cart fall down,
You'll still be the prettiest one in town.

Humpty Dumpty sat on a wall.
Humpty Dumpty had a great fall.
All the king's horses and
    all the king's men
Couldn't put Humpty
    together again.

Golden slumbers, kiss your eyes.
Smiles await you, when you rise.
Sleep, pretty darling, do not cry,
And I will sing a lullaby.